GET TO GRIPS
WITH SPANISH

Spanish Grammar for Beginners:

Por & Para

Julie Helliwell

ISBN: 9798864174654

For more information, contact
gettogripswithspanish@gmail.com

Each piece of the puzzle brings you closer to being able to see the full, glorious image. Don't stop now!

Table of Contents

Why I Wrote This Book 9

Why You Should Read This Book 11

Who This Book Is For 13

Chapter 1. Where Do I Start? 14

  Why Are Por & Para so Tricky?.. 14

Chapter 2. Por... 18

Chapter 3. Por – Time 20

Chapter 4. Por – Location.. 24

Chapter 5. Por – Gratitude/Apology.................................... 26

Chapter 6. Por – Means 27

Chapter 7. Por – In Exchange For 29

Chapter 8. Por – Passive Voice 30

Chapter 9. Por – For the Sake of 31

Chapter 10. Por – Distribution...................................... 32

Chapter 11. Por – Reason/Cause 33

Chapter 12. Por – On Behalf of 34

Chapter 13. Recap of Por... 35

Chapter 14. Expressions with Por..................................... 37

Chapter 15. Para 40

Chapter 16. Para – Destination 41

Chapter 17. Para – Contrast/Comparison 43

Chapter 18. Para – Employment.................................... 44

Chapter 19. Para – Deadline 45

Chapter 20. Para – Opinion 46

Chapter 21. Para – Objective/Purpose 47

Chapter 22. Recap of Para 50

Chapter 23. Expressions with Para 51

Chapter 24. Summary 52

Chapter 25. Grammar Glossary 53

About the Author 55

Other Books Available 56

One Last Thing 57

Why I Wrote This Book

I wrote this book (and the subsequent series) because learning Spanish grammar can be a total nightmare, and I want to save you from the torture!

I have literally spent *years* studying it, and just before I moved to Lanzarote six and a half years ago, I trained to teach English as a foreign language. Through this experience and subsequently working as an English teacher, I found that my biggest challenge was my lack of understanding of how English grammar works!

I don't know about you, as it'll depend on your age, but I can't remember studying any English grammar at school! I think we were taught what nouns, adjectives and verbs were, but that was about it! This doesn't matter one jot when you're speaking your native language, but when you start learning another or having to explain your own ... well, put it this way, other nationalities know a lot more about grammar than we do! They talk about all these different rules, constructs, and complex-sounding things that can, quite frankly, leave us English speakers feeling a bit stupid!

I actually love both Spanish and English grammar now–I can't get enough of it! I find that I'm often explaining it to the people I meet who are learning Spanish or English.

While my personal journey to Spanish fluency is not quite over, I feel that having a good grip on grammar is fundamental if you want to progress past holiday phrasebook Spanish.

There's absolutely nothing wrong with having no interest whatsoever in grammar, but if that's the case, this series of books isn't for you.

When teaching a foreign language, one rule is to only use that language. This has so many benefits, but there have been times when my fellow students and I would have done almost anything just to be given clarification or a simple definition in English.

That is why these books exist. I want to share tips, tricks and clear explanations in plain English so you can finally *Get to Grips with Spanish*–whichever part of it you're struggling with.

This series is written for learners of European Spanish. While there will be many similarities with Latin American Spanish, there will also be some differences, and to keep it simple, I have chosen to focus on Castilian Spanish.

This is the third book of the *Get to Grips with Spanish* series, but don't worry if you haven't read the first ones; they all stand alone. The QR code to the series link on Amazon is at the back of the book.

¡Buena suerte!

Why You Should Read This Book

If you have already read any of the *Get to Grips with Spanish* series, you can skip right ahead to Chapter 1 as you already know exactly why you're here.

If not, I don't know for sure, but I imagine you're considering this book because you want to know more about Spanish grammar as you recognise its importance. However (if you're anything like I was), you don't have much of a clue about how English works, so you get easily confused by all the complicated descriptions and rules!

I want to make those difficulties go away! My aim is to explain everything you need to know, but without the complexities that usually come hand-in-hand with learning grammar.

I will include references to the 'proper' terminology, so you know what things are called, as other people will use them (including your Spanish teacher and Spanish-speaking people who are studying English). However, the explanations will be as straightforward as I can make them so you can focus on speaking, rather than stressing out about grammar.

This particular book is focused on *por* and *para*, which, in the simplest terms, can both mean 'for' in English. However, as you will see, these two little words also have many other meanings. They can be the cause of much confusion when we have to decide

11

which to use.

In Chapter 25, there is a Grammar Glossary with a list of all the grammatical terms written in bold throughout the book, along with definitions and descriptions.

These short books are written as guides rather than exercise books. There are loads of online resources where you can find free quizzes to test yourself on what you have learned.

This book is part of a series. To let me know what other topics you would like me to help you with, please send me an email at gettogripswithspanish@gmail.com or contact me via the *Get to Grips with Spanish* Facebook page.

I have a plan for the order of books I am going to write, but if you contact me, your preference may jump the queue!

Who This Book Is For

This book is aimed at several groups of people:

- Ex-pats who have moved to Spain and want to immerse themselves in the local culture.
- People who intend to move to Spain.
- People who are already learning Spanish but are struggling to understand the grammar.
- People who want to take their Spanish to the next level.
- People who want to travel to Spanish-speaking countries where they have little understanding of English.

This book is not really written for people who already have a good understanding of grammar. If you fall into that category, it might seem very basic and boring. However, it will help you learn when to use *por* or *para*.

This book is a supplementary aid. It will not 'teach' you Spanish, but it will help you understand the grammatical concepts you are learning through other methods, e.g. classes, private tuition, mobile phone apps etc.

Chapter 1. Where Do I Start?

When doing the research to write this book, the more I read, the more notes I had to make and the more my brain questioned: "How can such tiny words cause so many problems?"

Why Are Por & Para so Tricky?

The reason *por* and *para* are such a challenge for English people learning Spanish is that they seem to have an infinite amount of meanings!

I'm not even joking! Well, perhaps I am overexaggerating slightly, but I thought I had pretty much nailed *por* and *para* until I started writing this. I confess I was wrong, but we are going to master them together, and I hope you'll have the 'aha' moment that I experienced!

The format of this book is that I'll take you through all of the uses for the **prepositions**, *por* and *para*. I am also going to include some common sayings and their meanings.

First up, just a quick explanation of what **prepositions** are. They are words that show the connections between the other words in a sentence. There are many types of prepositions. For example, there are **prepositions of place**, such as in the corner, at school, on the table, and prepositions of time, including in the morning, for hours, during the day, on Sundays, at night.

14

I plan to write a separate book on other prepositions, but for now, we'll just look at the tricky pair, *por* and *para*.

As a visual aid, I will use two images (and versions of them) in this book.

This image means *por:*

And this one means *para:*

I will explain the images in their relevant chapters.

We will also use two mnemonics as we go through the different categories for *por* and *para*. Rather than acronyms, like we had with *ser* and *estar*, in this book, we are going to use sentences.

At school, you perhaps used a mnemonic to remember the colours of the rainbow. Richard of York gave battle in vain. The first letter of each word helped memorise the order of the colours. ROYGBIV: red, orange, yellow, green, blue, indigo and violet.

For *por*, the sentence we'll use is **The legendary Goldilocks made incredible porridge from delicious rolled oats.** The associated categories are:

The	Time
Legendary	Location
Goldilocks	Gratitude/Apology
Made	Means
Incredible	In exchange for
Porridge	Passive
From	For the sake of
Delicious	Distribution
Rolled	Reason/Cause
Oats	On behalf of

For *para*, we will use the sentence: **Drinking coffee every day offers opportunities.** These are the categories for this mnemonic.

Drinking	Destination
Coffee	Contracts/Comparison
Every	Employment
Day	Deadline
Offers	Opinion
Opportunities	Objective/Purpose

If you're not a fan of mnemonics or wish to change these sentences, go ahead and make your own up. There are no rules – they just have to help you remember the categories. You can change the order of the letters or alter the descriptions and try to make your own acronym.

Chapter 2. Por

So, let's take another look at the image for *por*.

As you can see, this picture shows a wavy arrow that goes from left to right, towards a circle. The circle on the right is the end goal or result, whatever this is. The arrow is wavy because it is navigating around obstacles and travelling through them to get to its destination.

When thinking about using the word, *por*, one tip for some contexts is to think of it being a vague, roundabout way of achieving the goal.

Please note that this doesn't apply to all *por* categories, so I will add the image when it does.

Hopefully, this will all become much clearer as we now go through each meaning for *por* and look at loads of examples.

Here is a reminder of the mnemonic we're going to use for *por*:

The legendary Goldilocks made incredible porridge from delicious rolled oats.

The	Time
Legendary	Location
Goldilocks	Gratitude/Apology
Made	Means
Incredible	In exchange for
Porridge	Passive voice
From	For the sake of
Delicious	Distribution
Rolled	Reason/Cause
Oats	On behalf of

Let's go for it!   *¡Vamos por ello!*

Chapter 3. Por – Time

We're going to start with how to use *por* when referring to time. We can break this category down into three sub groups.

The first relates to **frequency** of actions, and in this case, *por* means per/each. We use it to describe how often something happens. Take a look at the wavy arrow below. Imagine that this is the timeframe, and the squares are the frequency that something is done.

English	Spanish
I go to the gym three times a (per) week.	Voy al gimnasio tres veces por semana.
She visits her parents once a month.	Ella visita a sus padres una vez por mes.
I do it twice a week.	Lo hago dos veces por semana.
We go to the cinema once a fortnight.	Vamos al cine una vez por quincena.
They go on holiday twice a year.	Ellos van de vacaciones dos veces por año.

The second is category is **duration/period of time,** and in these examples, *por* means <u>for</u>.

English	Spanish
I need a room for a week.	Necesito una habitación por una semana.
He needs your help for a day.	Él necesita tu ayuda por un día.
She read a magazine for two hours.	Ella leyó una revista por dos horas.
He is on holiday for two weeks.	Él está de vacaciones (por) dos semanas.*
I am staying here for a while.	Me quedo aquí (por) un rato.*
I was in London for a week.	Estuve en Londres (por) una semana.*

*Please note that *por* is often not used in this structure. Sometimes, it may be replaced by the word *durante*, but in mainland Spain, it is more likely to be missing entirely.

The rule around this relates to **intransitive verbs** that last for a period of time. These are verbs where the action only relates to the **subject** – there is no **direct object** in the sentence.

I was in London for a week.   *Estuve en Londres una semana.*

He lived in France for a year.   *Vivía en Francia un año.*

21

I worked here for two months.   *Trabajé aquí dos meses.*

It is important to know this because, as English speakers, we naturally want to add *por* into these phrases, but to sound more like a native, we need to cut it out!

When the verbs are **transitive**, i.e. they are done to a direct object, they are more likely to include the word *por* or *durante.*

He sang songs for an hour.   *Él cantó canciones por una hora.*

This is a lot to process, but I would advise you not to worry about it. If you do say *por* in these contexts, you won't be wrong, you'll just be adding unnecessary information! The more you speak to people, listen to the radio, audiobooks or podcasts or watch TV and films, the more you will notice and pick up on when to use it or not.

The third use is to talk about an **approximate or general timeframe**. In these examples, *por* means in/at.

English	Spanish
We're going to meet in the morning.	Vamos a quedar por la mañana.
I will arrive in the afternoon.	Llegaré por la tarde.
The bar is full in the evenings.	El bar está lleno por las noches.
I work (at) nights.	Trabajo por las noches.
They're going to deliver the sofa tomorrow morning.	Van a entregar el sofá mañana por la mañana.

So, just to recap, you use *por* to talk about time when referring to:

- frequency (per/each/a)
- duration (for)
- approximate timeframe (in/at)

Chapter 4. Por – Location

Going back to our mnemonic, **The legendary Goldilocks made incredible porridge from delicious rolled oats,** we're now onto legendary: **location.**

When using *por* in relation to location, it can be split into two categories: an approximate place and a movement in a location.

Both can be linked to this image.

Imagine that the wavy arrow is the route you are walking. If you want to talk about **approximate places**, using phrases such as <u>around</u>, <u>passing by</u> etc, this is where *por* comes in.

English	Spanish
It's around here.	Está por aquí.
Where are you?	¿Dónde estás?
I'm passing by the church.	Voy por la iglesia.
Is there a bank around here?	¿Hay un banco por aquí?

The second category of location refers to **movement** in a place.

Again, imagine the wavy arrow relates to the journey. If you want to use phrases such as <u>walk around,</u> <u>go through</u> etc, this is how you do it.

English	Spanish
Every morning I run through the park.	Cada mañana, corro por el parque.
The taxi driver drove through the city.	El taxista conduzco por la ciudad.
They walk around the forest.	Ellos caminan por el bosque.
We passed through France to get to Germany.	Pasamos por Francia para llegar a Alemania.

So, just to recap, you use *por* to talk about location when referring to:

- an approximate place (around, passing by)

- movement in a location (around/through)

Chapter 5. Por – Gratitude/Apology

We now move onto **Goldilocks** in our mnemonic, meaning **gratitude**. This category also covers making apologies and offering condolences.

When saying thank you for something or apologising, *por* is the equivalent of <u>for</u> in English. Finally, a simple one!

English	Spanish
Thank you for coming.	Gracias por venir.*
Thanks for your patience.	Gracias por tu paciencia.
Sorry for being late.	Perdona por llegar tarde.
I apologise for the misunderstanding.	Te pido disculpas por el malentendido.
My deepest condolences for your loss.	Mi más sentido pésame por tu perdida.

TOP TIP ALERT!

*Whenever you say *Gracias por* and you want to use a verb e.g. calling, coming, asking etc, rather than using the **gerund** (verb + ing) as we do in English, in Spanish, they use the **infinitive** (the full verb). *Gracias por llamar/venir/preguntar etc.*

26

Chapter 6. Por – Means

You might get sick of this, but to make sure you remember it, here's our *por* mnemonic again: **The legendary Goldilocks made incredible porridge from delicious rolled oats.** We're now looking at using *por* to talk about **means**, and there are two categories: **communication** and **transportation**.

Both categories can be linked to this image, with the wavy line being the means of communication or transportation that connect one thing to another:

In relation to means of communication, *por* means <u>by</u>, <u>via</u> or <u>on</u>.

English	Spanish
I called him on the phone.	Le llamé a él por teléfono.
Send it to me by/via email.	Mándamelo por correo electrónico.
She will send the location of the party via WhatsApp.	Ella mandará la ubicación de la fiesta por WhatsApp.
They communicated by code.	Ellos comunicaron por código.

When related to transportation, *por* usually means <u>by</u>.

English	Spanish
The package will be delivered by boat.	El paquete será entregado por barco.
The island is accessible by plane.	La isla está accesible por avión.
She crosses London on the underground/tube.	Ella cruza Londres por metro.
Travelling by sea is slower than by air.	Viajar por mar es más lento que por aire.

Please note that when **you** are travelling, you can also say *en tren, avión etc. En* is one of the prepositions that I will cover in another book as it can mean by/in/on, depending on usage and context.

I prefer to travel by train.   *Prefiero viajar en tren.*

So, just to recap, you use *por* to talk about means when referring to:

- communication (by/via/on)
- movement in a location (around/through)

Chapter 7. Por – In Exchange For

Now we've reached the **incredible** part of our mnemonic phrase. When using *por* to talk about an **exchange** we have made, it corresponds to the word <u>for</u>.

Exchanges can refer to paying for something (exchanging money for an item), or swapping things, as you see in this diagram.

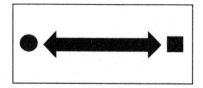

English	Spanish
I paid €5 (in exchange) for lunch.	Pagué 5€ por el almuerzo.
Can I exchange this dress for a larger size?	¿Puedo cambiar este vestido por una talla más grande?
It cost €80 for two nights.	Costó 80€ por dos noches.
She offered me €20 for my watch.	Ella me ofreció 20€ por mi reloj.
I can't believe you paid €100 for that!	¡No puedo creer que pagaras 100€ por ello!

Chapter 8. Por – Passive Voice

So, Goldilock's **porridge** relates to using *por* with the **passive voice**. "What on earth is the passive voice?" I hear you cry. Well, at least, that's what I thought when I first heard of it.

In a sentence that is written or spoken in the passive voice, the action is more important than the subject. Passive voice is used more commonly in writing than speaking, and you will recognise it when you see it. A good way to think about it is that something has been done/caused <u>by</u> someone or something.

English	Spanish
The Starry Night was painted by Vincent van Gogh.	La Noche Estrella fue pintada por Vincent van Gogh.
Romeo and Juliet was written by Shakespeare.	Romeo y Julieta fue escrita por Shakespeare.
My car was stolen by a thief.	Mi coche fue robado por un ladrón.
A lot of damage was caused by the flood.	Mucho daño fue causado por la inundación.
A prize was won by the boy.	Un premio fue ganado por el niño.

Chapter 9. Por – For the Sake of

If you want to say something using the phrase **for the sake of**, you also use *por*.

English	Spanish
Eat for the sake of eating.	Comer por comer.
I do it for the sake of my family.	Lo hago por mi familia.
Many parents stay together for the sake of their children.	Muchos padres se quedan juntos por sus niños.
I don't need it. I'm just buying it for the sake of buying something.	No lo necesito. Solo lo estoy comprando por comprar algo.

A slight variation to this is to say *por el bien de*, which means for the good of.

English	Spanish
He stopped drinking for the good of his health.	Dejó de beber por el bien de su salud.
We save water for the good of the planet.	Ahorramos agua por el bien del planeta.

Chapter 10. Por – Distribution

We're now onto the D in our phrase, **The legendary Goldilocks made incredible porridge from <u>delicious</u> rolled oats.** It relates to using *por* with **distribution**, meaning how things are divided, and is generally <u>per</u> in English.

This image shows how things might be distributed between people or places.

English	Spanish
One drink per person.	Una bebida por persona.
The maximum is two boxes per person.	El máximo es dos cajas por persona.
The capacity is four people per room.	El aforo es cuatro personas por habitación.
The limit is three hours per visit.	El límite es tres horas por visita.

Chapter 11. Por – Reason/Cause

When using *por* as a **reason** or **cause** for something, a good way do this is to think of the words <u>because of</u>. In some cases, <u>for</u> is more common.

English	Spanish
Because of him, we're late.	Por él, llegamos tarde.
Because of that, I left.	Por eso, me fui.
I did it because of (for) my family.	Lo hice por mi familia.
The dog barked because of the cat.	El perro ladró por el gato.
The ice cream melted because of the sun.	El helado se derritió por el sol.
He wanted the promotion because of (for) the salary increase.	Él quería el ascenso por el aumento de sueldo.

In these instances, *por* indicates a direct causal link between things. One thing wouldn't happen without the other.

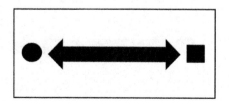

Chapter 12. Por – On Behalf of

We have reached the **oats** of our sentence! If we use *por* to talk about doing something **on someone's behalf,** in English, this is likely to replace <u>for/instead of.</u>

English	Spanish
I'm working for (instead of) Chris – he's sick today.	Trabajo por Chris – hoy está enfermo.
As Ronaldo was injured, a substitute played for him.	Como Ronaldo estuvo lesionado, un sustituto jugó por él.
My boss is on holiday, so I have to work at the weekend for him.	Mi jefe está de vacaciones, así que tengo que trabajar el fin de semana por él.
I speak for all my family when I say congratulations.	Hablo por toda mi familia cuando digo felicidades.
Can you please attend that meeting on my behalf?	¿Puedes asistir a esa reunión por mí, por favor?

One thing is represented by another, as you can see in this image.

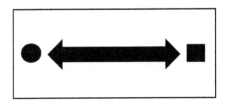

Chapter 13. Recap of Por

So let's do a quick recap and condense the information we have just covered into a table. Remember the sentence?

The legendary Goldilocks made incredible porridge from delicious rolled oats.

Category	English meaning	Spanish example
Time (frequency)	per/each/a	Lo hago dos veces por semana.
Time (duration)	for	Voy a leer (por) un rato.
Time (approx. period)	in/at	Llegaré por la noche.
Location (approx. place)	around/ passing by	Está por aquí. Voy por la iglesia.
Location (movement in a place)	around/through	Cada mañana, corro por el parque.
Gratitude/Apology	for	Gracias por venir.
Means (communication)	by/via/on	Le llamé a él por teléfono.
Mean (of transportation)	by	La isla está accesible por avión.
In exchange for	for	Pagué 5€ por el almuerzo.

Passive voice	by	Romeo y Julieta fue escrita por Shakespeare.
For the sake of	for the sake of	Comer por comer.
Distribution	per	Una bebida por persona.
Reason/Cause	because of/for	Por él, llegamos tarde.
On behalf of	for/instead of	Trabajo por Chris – hoy está enfermo.

Chapter 14. Expressions with Por

There are lots of handy little expression that are commonly used with *por* and *para*. Here are a few *por* ones to get you started.

English	Spanish
all the time	cada dos por tres
almost	por poco
apparently (by the look of it)	por lo visto
at least	por lo menos
at that time	por aquel entonces
at times	por momentos
barely	por los pelos
because	porque
by chance	por casualidad
by the way	por cierto
completely/absolutely	por completo
everywhere	por todas partes
for the first/last time	por primera/última vez
finally	por fin
for example	por ejemplo
for nothing/easily	por menos de nada
for now/so far	por ahora
for the good of	por el bien de
in advance	por adelantado

just in case	por si acaso
luckily	por suerte
nowhere	por ningún lado
percent	por ciento
please	por favor
separately	por separado
thanks to (sb)/through (sb)	por medio de (alguien)
that's why	por eso
therefore	por lo tanto
unfortunately	por desgracia
whether you like it or not	por las buenas o por las malas
why	por qué
word for word	palabra por palabra

There are also a few verbs than use *por* as their adjoining preposition. Here are some examples. It's on my to-do list to write a whole book about verbs and their connecting prepositions, so keep an eye out for that in the future.

English	Spanish
to apologise for	disculparse por
to ask about	preguntar por
to be in favour of	estar por
to begin with	comenzar por (o con)
to exchange for	cambiar por
to fight for	luchar por
to leave via	salir por
to pay for	pagar por
to pray for	rezar por
to travel by	viajar por
to start with	comenzar por
to vote for	votar por
to worry about	preocuparse por

Chapter 15. Para

Ok! Now, let's move on to the other tricky little word: *para.* The image we're going to use (and versions of) is this one. As you can see, it's more straightforward and direct than the *por* image.

Here is a reminder of the mnemonic we're going to use for the *para* categories:

Drinking coffee every day offers opportunities.

Drinking	Destination
Coffee	Contracts/Comparison
Every	Employment
Day	Deadline
Offers	Opinion
Opportunities	Objective/Purpose

Ok, here we go!

Chapter 16. Para – Destination

So, the **drinking** part of our sentence relates to **destination**, which can be a physical place or a recipient of something. Basically, it's where someone or something ends up, hence the image. When using *para* to refer to a **destination**, think of the words to/for.

English	Spanish
I am going to England next week.	Voy para Inglaterra la semana que viene.
The train to Madrid leaves in ten minutes.	El tren para Madrid sale en diez minutos.
She drives to London via Manchester.	Ella conduce para Londres por Manchester.
These toys are for your children.	Estos juguetes son para tus hijos.
Who are the flowers for?	¿Para quién son las flores?
This gift is for you.	Este regalo es para ti.

Para can also indicate movement, meaning <u>towards/to</u>, rather than referring to a final destination. Imagine you are running late and someone calls you, asking where you are. You might want to give an approximate location to indicate how close you are.

It's worth noting that *para* may be replaced with *hacia* in these situations.

English	Spanish
I'm on the main street, walking towards the bank.	Estoy en la calle principal, caminando para el banco.
The thief is going towards the door! Stop him!	¡El ladrón va para la puerta! ¡Deténlo!
I am heading south.	Voy para el sur.
I'm on my way (I'm heading in your direction.)	Voy para allá.

So, just to recap, you use *para* to talk about destination when referring to:

- a place (to)

- a person receiving something (for)

- movement (towards)

Chapter 17. Para – Contrast/Comparison

In our phrase, **Drinking coffee every day offers opportunities**, coffee deals with **contrast/comparison**. It is usually in relation to an existing expectation we have of something. When using *para* to talk about how something doesn't meet our expectations, it replaces <u>for</u> in English.

English	Spanish
For June, it's really cold.	Para ser junio, hace mucho frío.
For how expensive it is, the quality is very low.	Para lo cara que es, la calidad es muy baja.
For a young girl, she has a powerful voice.	Para ser una jovencita, tiene una voz poderosa.
For the time of year, the flights are much more expensive than normal.	Para la época del año, los vuelos son mucho más caros de lo normal.

.

Chapter 18. Para – Employment

When using *para* to talk about work and who you or someone else is **employed** by, it also replaces the word <u>for</u> in English.

In Chapter 12, we used *por* when we were working **on behalf of** someone else (in their place) for a specific reason, but with *para*, it refers to the company or person who pays your wages. It also covers any voluntary work that you do.

English	Spanish
I work for a furniture company.	Trabajo para una empresa de muebles.
I don't work for anyone. I am retired.	Trabajo para nadie. Estoy jubilado.
She works for her family business.	Ella trabaja para su empresa familiar.
He worked for a global corporation for 15 years, but now is self-employed.	Él trabajó para una corporación global por 15 años, pero ahora es autónomo.
She volunteers for an animal charity.	Ella es voluntaria para una organización benéfica.
He used to work for a bank.	Él trabajaba para un banco.

Chapter 19. Para – Deadline

The **day** in our phrase, **Drinking coffee every day offers opportunities** means **deadline**. When referring to **deadlines** using *para,* in English, this would be <u>by/for/no later than</u>.

In the image, the spot is the deadline date and the line indicates the time leading up to submission.

English	Spanish
I need this report no later than Monday.	Necesito este informe para el lunes.
You have to submit your application by the end of the week.	Tienes que entregar tu solicitud para el fin de la semana.
I have to pay my rent by noon.	Tengo que pagar el alquilar para mediodía.
He has to improve his Spanish by August.	Él tiene que mejorar su español para agosto.
I want to move house by the end of summer.	Quiero mudarme de casa para el final del verano.

Chapter 20. Para – Opinion

The first O in our phrase, **Drinking coffee every day offers opportunities** means **opinion**. When using *para* to give or ask for an **opinion**, this substitutes <u>for/to</u> in English.

It can also mean <u>in my opinion</u>, or in the opinion of whoever is being addressed/referred to.

In this instance, the line in the image constitutes the opinion, and the dot is who is receiving it.

English	Spanish
For me, it's too expensive.	Para mí, es demasiado caro.
In your opinion, which is better?	Para ti, ¿cuál es mejor?
In my boss's opinion, we can do better.	Para mi jefe, podemos hacerlo mejor.
For us, a beach holiday is the best way to relax.	Para nosotros, un día en la playa es la mejor manera de relajarse.

Chapter 21. Para – Objective/Purpose

We've made it to the end of our phrase, **Drinking coffee every day offers opportunities!** When using *para* as an **objective** or **purpose** for something, a good way do this is to think of the phrase <u>in order to/to</u>. In these cases, the arrow indicates the thing being done to achieve the goal.

English	Spanish
I avoid coffee before going to bed in order to sleep well.	Evito el café antes de acostarme para poder dormir bien.
I work so much in order to earn more money.	Trabajo tanto para ganar más dinero.
He is learning Spanish in order to be understood.	Él aprende español para ser entendido.
She studied to pass the exam.	Ella estudió para aprobar el examen.
They worked together to achieve their dreams.	Ellos trabajaban junto para lograr sus sueños.

Also in this category, *para* is used to explain the benefits/disadvantages of something, either in general or for specific people. It also indicates the usefulness or function of something that is to be used.

English	Spanish
Take honey and lemon to get rid of your cough.	Toma miel y limón para deshacerse de la tos.
Doing sudoku is good for improving memory.	Hacer sudoku es bueno para mejorar la memoria.
Smoking is bad for your health.	Fumar es malo para la salud.
The game is for (to be used by) children.	El juego es para niños.
We need a room for two (to be used by two people).	Necesitamos una habitación para dos.
Can I book a table for six (to be used by six people)?	¿Puedo reservar una mesa para seis?
Designed for small dogs.	Deseñados para perros pequeños.
Written for teenagers.	Escrito para adolescentes.
I did it for my family (for their benefit).	Lo hice para mi familia.

So, just to recap, you use *para* when referring to:

- an objective/purpose (in order to)

- benefits/functionality (for/to be used by)

48

Let's just take a quick closer look at that last example: *Lo hice para mi familia.* As you will hopefully have realised while reading this book, *por* and *para* usually indicate quite different things. Once you learn the categories, practice and notice them, I am confident you will naturally select the correct one.

However, in Chapter 11, we had a very similar example: *Lo hice por mi familia.* When using *por* here, it means <u>because of</u> – they were the **reason** I did it.

I want to explore this nuance a little more because with phrases like these, we can use both prepositions, but they have slightly different meanings.

Imagine a film about the son of a major mafia gangster. (Bizarre, I know, but stick with me!) He wants to prove to his father that he can take over the family business, so he commits a terrible crime. If he says *Lo hice por mi familia*, it can mean two things: 1) he did it <u>because of</u> his family (it was his duty), or 2) he did it <u>on behalf of</u> his family (in their name/honour).

However, if he says, *Lo hice para mi familia,* he means he did it to benefit them (perhaps they were in danger).

Chapter 22. Recap of Para

So let's do a quick recap of the categories for **Drinking coffee every day offers opportunities.**

Category	English meaning	Spanish example
Destination (place)	to	El tren para Madrid sale en diez minutos.
Destination (person)	for	Este regalo es para ti.
Destination (movement)	towards/to	Voy para el sur.
Contrast/Comparison	for	Para ser junio, hace mucho frío.
Employment	for	Trabajo para una empresa de muebles.
Deadline	by/for/no later than	Necesito este informe para el lunes.
Opinion	for	Para mí, es demasiado caro.
Objective/Purpose	in order to	Ella estudió para aprobar el examen.
Objective/Purpose	for (to be used by)	Quiero una mesa para dos, por favor.

Chapter 23. Expressions with Para

As we saw in Chapter 13, many commonly used expressions contain *por* and *para*. Here are some *para* ones to add to your ever-expanding Spanish vocabulary.

English	Spanish
By that time/by then	para entonces
for a change	para variar
for another time	para otra vez
for nothing/not at all	para nada
forever	para siempre
For what reason/purpose?	¿Para qué?
I'm on my way.	Voy para allá.
It's no big deal.	No es para tanto.
so that/in order that	para que
to be about to	estar para
to start/finish	para empezar/terminar

Chapter 24. Summary

Congratulations! You have reached the end, and you now know all there is to know about the difference between *por* and *para*, and when to use which!

All that's left to do now is to put your new knowledge into practice. If you don't have anyone to speak Spanish to, keep your eyes and ears open for any time you see or hear *por* or *para* being used. When this happens, if it's possible, pause and think about which category it fits into.

I don't ever want these grammar rules to become a block that get in the way of speaking; believe me, I've been there, done that, got a few T-shirts! So don't feel that you need to do this mental categorisation too often. However, now that you know which word is correct, over time, your brain will start making the connections, and will begin to provide you with the right one instinctively.

Chapter 25. Grammar Glossary

Term	E.g.	Explanation	Spanish term	Chap
Preposition	por, para	Words that show the connections between the other words in a sentence.	Preposición	1
Intransitive verb		A verb where the action relates to the subject. There is no direct object.	Verbo intransitivo	3
Subject		Generally, the person or thing in the sentence that is actioning the verb.	Sujeto	3
Direct object		Generally, the recipient of the action in the sentence.	Objeto directo	3
Transitive verb		A verb where the action is done to a direct object.	Verbo transitivo	3
Gerund		When you add -ing to a verb when referring to an ongoing	Gerundio	5

		action.		
Infinitive		The full verb, which ends in ar, ir or er in Spanish.	Infinitivo	5
Passive voice		When the subject receives the action of the sentence.	Voz pasiva	8

About the Author

JULIE HELLIWELL was born and raised in East Yorkshire but moved to Lanzarote in 2017. This relocation and subsequent delving deeper into the world of learning another language changed her life completely. She currently works as a musician, editor and translator (from Spanish to English). Julie is the author of the series *Get to Grips with Spanish*. You can contact her via email at <u>gettogripswithspanish@gmail.com</u> or through the *Get to Grips with Spanish* Facebook page.

Other Books Available

Get to Grips with Spanish: Masculine & Feminine, Singular & Plural

Get to Grips with Spanish: Ser & Estar (To Be)

To purchase either of these books, go to the *Get to Grips with Spanish* series page on Amazon via the QR code below.

Coming Soon:

Get to Grips with Spanish: Verbs with Prepositions

Get to Grips with Spanish: Pronouns

Get to Grips with Spanish: Adverbs

Get to Grips with Spanish: Adjectives

Get to Grips with Spanish: Reflexive Verbs

And many more …

One Last Thing ...

If you enjoyed this book or found it helpful, I'd be very grateful if you'd post a short review on Amazon. Your support really makes a difference, and I read all the reviews personally to get your feedback and make this book and the series even better.

If you'd like to leave a review then all you need to do is click the review link on this book's Amazon page which you can access via the QR code on the previous page.

Thanks again for reading, and I hope you come back for the next *Get to Grips with Spanish* book!

Best wishes,

Julie

Printed in Great Britain
by Amazon